REQUIEM IN RHYME

VOLUME 1

DUSTIN EDWARDS

Columbus, Ohio

This book is a work of fiction. The names, characters and events in this book are the products of the author's imagination or are used fictitiously. Any similarity to real persons living or dead is coincidental and not intended by the author.

The views and opinions expressed in this book are solely those of the author and do not reflect the views or opinions of Gatekeeper Press. Gatekeeper Press is not to be held responsible for and expressly disclaims responsibility of the content herein.

REQUIEM IN RHYME

Published by **Gatekeeper Press**
2167 Stringtown Rd, Suite 109
Columbus, OH 43123-2989
www.GatekeeperPress.com

Copyright © 2022 by **Dustin Edwards**

All rights reserved. Neither this book, nor any parts within it may be sold or reproduced in any form or by any electronic or mechanical means, including information storage and retrieval systems, without permission in writing from the author. The only exception is by a reviewer, who may quote short excerpts in a review.

The editorial work for this book is entirely the product of the author. Gatekeeper Press did not participate in and is not responsible for any aspect of this element.

Copyright for the image:
iStockphoto.com/Joshua Bennetts

Library of Congress Control Number: 2022931662

ISBN (paperback): 9781662925580
eISBN: 9781662925597

REQUIEM IN RHYME

VOLUME 1

FOREWORD

Poetry is an odd literary craft that hearkens to music and carries over its tempo and expressive pleasure. The structural design is crucial and that means good writing of such variety requires an adroit craftsman be at the workbench.

Definitive and evocative with every stanza, these compositions paint the portrait of a person I know to be of that caliber. Insomuch as a part of the human experience can be conveyed by what we describe as poignant, Edwards vividly delves into and out of his psyche to deliver a tumult of misery and turmoil.

Despite that, he is consistently determined to pose the structure of that struggle as something that's worth enduring. The pen is mightiest when the skilled hand reiterates fear, uncertainty, and doubt with a redemptive hope that these are not all that need find us as feelings in life. While some of these may be more easily related to, they're all worth their time to read over and contemplate.

What great prose does to tell an endearing tale, poetry acts to light the flames to our minds and hearts. With any luck, you'll find these a beacon to be a better, more fully found version of yourself; they did that for me at least.

B.C. Mitchell

CONTENTS

This One is for Me	8
Beautiful Sadness	10
The Well	12
Nostalgia Currently	13
Cadence	14
A to Z	15
The Devil in the Mirror	16
Tide	18
This is My Elegy	19
Dopamine	20
There's Always Something	21
Permanent You	22
The Contrarian	23
Alone in the Dark	25
I Can Breathe	26
True Terror	27
Honest Thoughts	28

Honester Thoughts	30		*Living on the Inside*	61
Broken Brain	32		*Sunset Fades*	63
Escape Your Brain	34		*Thinking Without Thinking*	64
100 Proof	36			
The Prelude	38			
True Addiction	39			
Waking Up	41			
Depression	42			
I Love You	43			
Bottle Metaphor	45			
What's Wrong	48			
I Need Help	50			
Satisfaction of Delusion	52			
Final Moment	53			
Angel and Demon	55			
Fear	57			
Deeply Flawed	59			

This One is for Me

When words hit the page, it sets me free
But most of them aren't the ones that let me be
The me that gets comfortable enough to read them back
Recheck diction in triplicate because my shit is whack

So this time the prose is strictly my own
Welcome to the process, step into my home
I feel the most alive with a book, quiet, alone
Or on a long drive, with the pavement to roam

Extroverted introvert with weight on his chest
Giving back to people is when I'm at my best
Deeply introspective and a colossal fucking mess
I apologize for all the times I cause people stress

Give me a pen, or maybe a knife
I'll create you a little slice of my life
We'll laugh and be jovial; share a moment or two
But after all that, it's time for me to review

All the words and all the jokes
And every mistake I've made
Different strokes for different folks
I wish to the back I could fade

Death occupies my thoughts more than I like
Recurrent issue, just a cranium riding its bike
I'm not in a hurry, but the 'what if' is real
Final peace and quiet seems like a good deal

I say things most won't; it's just how I'm wired
I drink too much, I'm irreverent, and constantly tired
But I love you more than your brain will allow
You can have the shirt off my back and the sweat from my brow

I wrote this poem for exclusively me
Because it's been a hot minute since my voices agreed
Sometimes you get grounded before you launch into space
The ground level starts every staircase

I'll get back to the words for you in the morrow
But this piece was my lexical summit of Kilimanjaro
I needed catharsis and all that it offers
To allow me to go back to filling your coffers

With awful rhymes, worse insight
Bad puns and inferior jokes
Or maybe some odd foresight
This one was for me, a happiness coax

Now I'll smile again, and hope you follow suit
Lay a spade or a heart, the game is yours to uproot
Do nice things for yourself now and then
Take the losses with solace and they lead to a win

Beautiful Sadness

The tear forms in the corner of my eye
The sadness lets me know I'm alive
Channeled emotions spawn the cry
The beauty in caring is what helps me thrive

Some confer weakness to emotional turmoil
But I find strength in expressing empathy
Care about someone with no recoil
These words my obtuse sympathy

Melancholy, morose, downtrodden, gloomy or glum
None of these are concepts with a permanent outcome
And none are things you should always run from
Sadness can be managed and if needed, overcome

Not all sadness comes in negative forms
Some of those feelings spawn cranial storms
With fresh creativity and perspective reform
Touching human insights to share and inform

I start to breathe quickly, and my heart starts to race
My brain places itself in another human's place
I feel all they feel, and it shows on my face
It motivates kind action, it's my one saving grace

Sadness is ugly; inherently cruel
Mascara is running, grey matter cesspool
The beautiful thing about terribly sad
Is that being a human isn't half bad

So, you cry massive tears
And you weep and you sob
Because others have fears
That make your loving heart throb

Not all situations may have a fix
But your beautiful sadness puts you in the mix
To relate to others while your emotions affix
To some bad ass humans, and not just for kicks

Be sad for an hour, a day or a year
There's nothing wrong with needing to clear
Your head with a beer, some cheer or a tear
Your sexy ass sadness enlarges your sphere

The Well

It's dark down here
The damp invades
No one can hear
As the fear cascades

No recollection of falling in
Just trepidation of the state you're in
Search for a handhold, all in vain
Alone in a hole with just your pain

You cry out for help, but no one comes
Just the beat of your heart in your eardrums
You play out all the inevitable outcomes
All of the parts, but none of the sums

No rope, no ladder, no Lassie or savior
Just contemplation of self and your own misbehavior
You wonder who even dug this hell
But you know the answer far too well

The sun has gone down, and you glance at the moon
You want it all to end, but it would be too soon
More failed attempts to climb, but none opportune
You settle into the well and embrace your cocoon

The hole becomes home, the only thing you know
Albeit awfully slow, love of the well starts to grow
You become part of the pit, no above or below
You realize the depression is the actual plateau

Nostalgia Currently ─────────────

I miss tickle fights and tent blanket nights
I miss dino bites and that kid magazine Highlights
I missed where lack of civil rights created last rites
I missed the point where we lost the Bill of Rights

I miss grass stains and errant mud tracks
I miss paper planes and pudding lunch packs
I missed that financial gains are remiss of most tax
I missed that the color of your skin absolves most acts

I miss recess frolicking free and losing the spelling bee
I miss a cushion whoopee and thinking death comes at thirty-three
I missed decades of spending recklessly hoping fiat sets us free
I missed centuries of debauchery, forcing weak to take a knee

I miss the awkward movie first date, kiss the orthodontist can't hate
I miss the sex-ed menstruate, penetrate, permeate. I lied. Obliviate.
I missed where those who aspirate are required to designate
I missed where being able to acclimate to any human state made you substrate

I miss choosing a major for money, and finding hobbies for pleasure
I miss chasing the easter bunny, the end of the leisure; no treasure
I missed that all the things that I hated were the person I had created
I missed that with all the things I have done, not even prodigal son

I miss stupid texts because I lost sight of things that matter
I miss laughing at such depths, peace, and friendships to tatter
I missed my locus shift, but I will proceed with sanity
I missed the profanity of acting without fucking humanity

Cadence

They teach you to drum your own beat
But don't teach about all the heat
That a different rhythm will bring
No matter the song that you sing

Just have to keep tapping your foot
Or flames turn your carbon to soot
The way your head bobs without noise
Is the cornerstone of your poise

They'll use words like special/unique
While omitting the chanting of freak
Normalcy becomes an ethereal goal
That if gained brings trauma to soul

If four-four isn't your signature time
Quarters don't add up, drop a few dimes
Nickel the eighths with a sprinkle of thyme
32nd trip's when you find the right clime

That's weather, ends in e
Mountaineering, ends with b
Get used to the latter one
Extra rungs on your ladder son

Don't put your drumming sticks down
Or drown the songs in your head
You may be the laughingstock of the town
Don't give in, stay true to your cadence instead

A to Z

Alphabetize
Butterflies
Canonize
Digitize

Eagle eyes
Flimsy fries
Golden guise
Hellish highs

Idealize
Jeopardize
Kingdomize
Lengthy lies

Mobilize
Normalize
Ostracize
Privatize

Qualify
Risky rye
Sexy sigh
Thickish thigh

Understood
Victimhood
Womanhood

X is shite
Y as well
Zoomy zoom zoom zoom

The Devil in the Mirror

They call it a looking glass
But are you happy with what you're looking at?
Sometimes you may want to pass
If you're feeling sad or feeling fat

I always thought mirrors told the truth
Knowledge taught to me in my youth
Sometimes mirrors expose the lie
That you've placed inside mind's eye

Light reflected, scientifically proved
True human reflection often removed
Due to stereotypes and magazines
Or Instagram and TV screens

The devil in the mirror isn't you
Stems from the bullshit I got fed too
The devil is only in your head
Shatter mirrors and memories; the future's ahead

We chastise ourselves for past mistakes
While we wash our hands and do what it takes
To rid our existence of all infection
Often avoiding our beautiful reflection

I've been drunk and so very high
Staring at the mirror, pondering why
I'm the devil and a sinner
Not the champion or a winner

We must learn to live our lives
Be good to folks, hand out high fives
I know that's a dumbass, corny line
But this is my poem and I find it fine

None of your mirrors hold a devil
They hold humans who kick ass at a level
That can't be measured on an evil scale
So long as you spend your purpose well

Tide

The moon rises, but never falls
My life preaches ebbs and floes
The almanac can make the calls
But risk teaches how it goes

Spent lots of years watching
Waters change their minds
So many lessons notching
With feelings of all kinds

This cycle, unlike another
Let's us examine all the past
Gravity creates a brother
But the fish contain contrast

Iodine jest for the allergic folk
And this topic stabs at a soul
Ideas break and cook like a yolk
But all concepts end up in a bowl

My head is swimming
No one is winning
I'm tired of waking up crying
I've not yet conquered the tide
But you can bet your ass I'm trying

This is My Elegy

Death is a focus, perspective relief
Life loses locus, inevitable grief
Not the flavor of mortality today
In this hour, reflection on life decay

Terminate the need to be socially normal
Suffocate the breath of doubt in your talent
Eliminate some ingrained need to be formal
Abolish the notion that all heroes are gallant

Invalidate the premise that success is a myth
Suspend the idea that your work is for naught
Overrule the motion that your thoughts lack pith
Adjourn the meetings with your negative thought

Retire the theory that you've nothing else to give
Deregister the proposition that you don't deserve to live
Curtail the concept that you're an island, alone
Abandon the memory of every shot blown

These are the things that strangle your life
This is our society, negative feedback, rife
The demise of the lot reduces the strife
But it must be you wielding the knife

It may sound insurmountable
One step at a time
Your options uncountable
Always in your prime

The new you begins with the collapse of the old
From the ashes, cold, rise fiery artworks of gold
This is my elegy, my beautiful focus on loss
Death to the things in my life which are dross

Dopamine

When the dopamine doesn't hit
And the thoughts don't seem to quit
You double down and recommit
To write the shit only you can spit

I won't lie to myself again
Been scared to wield the pen
Like the seven to the ten
Split the bowl and win the zen

Tip the bottle less, inhale a little more
Brain still a mess, each breath muffles the roar
A vice game of chess, the pour or the score
Is it really progress? Or am I the whore in this war

Probably the latter, and a cheap one at that
A thousand notions scatter like the flight of a bat
To the page from grey matter, yet most fall flat
Ramblings of a hatter, a mad mercurial cat

Right the ship, a broken notion echoes in my head
Add a double you and craft it, it'll play, or you'll be dead
No rites or incantations can spare me from this dread
But writing out these words is a path I'll always tread

There's Always Something

There's pain
Then there's arguing with your brain
Sipping every bottle to alter what courses through your veins
Knowing that a smile is a thing you can't attain

There's fear
Then there's feeling like there's nothing for you here
Swallowing every pill trying to disappear
Just to wake and hear medical beeping in your ears

There's hate
Then there's despair at the world that you create
Perpetuating cycles you'd love to just cessate
But it's how you acclimate to the things you can't abate

There's love
Then there's this falsity that there's something more above
Reading every book as if knowledge is the shove
That will solve all the problems the world needs rid of

There's sadness
Then there's driving 5,000 miles to distract you from your madness
Finding new ways to absolve you of the drabness
But knowing nothing will ever really alter status

There's nothing
Then there's the idea of all creation
Wondering why you've been given this duration
Feeling less than human in your constant rumination

Permanent You

The permanent you is always in queue
Like Shakespeare, taming your shrew
Smoke in the chimney, rise through the flue
Become the best being you ever knew

Doesn't make it easy, morons make it painful
But support makes the trials seem very gainful
A laugh and a hug, a weird shoulder shrug
People matter and they're a tick with a bug

Commit to being better, that's all we can do
And I won't assume to even know the real you
But I find being genuine is a DNA glue
And I'm repurposing myself to be true

So let's be the best us, no creature can contest us
When we're the stressed us, reflect on the blessed us
There will be distressed us; probably oppressed us
But we are the progressed us; and no soul can suppress us

Words written for me, but I hope dumb diction makes you see
That all is not lost and there's no enduring guilty plea
I can't know what holds the lock to your key
But I know for sure I want you on this planet with me

The Contrarian

Think a little different, act a little weird
Be a bit indifferent, end up being feared
The box was never a thing that applied to you
You questioned everything to find what's true

You read, you watch; you stop and you pause
You analyze the info, each sentence, every clause
Fall in line, be normal, do what they say
You do so for a while, then you find a new way

You pick up the books you weren't to read
You watch all the things you weren't to see
Inside of your head is planted a seed
Are these self-important people programming me?

A man with emotion, a woman bad ass and strong
Start up the commotion and show them they're wrong
Forget everyone who tries to box you in
Ignore the hatred, it can't help you win

Luther, Edison, Tesla, King
These dudes weren't normal, but they make your mind ping
Ginsburg, Barton, Tubman, Nightingale
These ladies weren't normal, but they create the human tale

Hamilton, Lincoln, Robinson, X
Gentlemen who showed us what could come next
Anthony, O'Connor, Ride, Sacajawea
Women who showed us how thinking can free ya

Take heart in knowing we're not all the same
Appreciate the fact that you're using your brain
There's always a new way to play the same game
The best slabs of meat are cut against the grain

Be humble and honest, but true in your actions
The simpleminded will always have their reactions
They're not on your level, lacking mental transactions
Write amazing headlines, never print retractions

'Contrary to popular belief' is just what we need
To help our fellow lifeforms succeed
In this life we live and share together forever
We contrarians are birds of a feather

That stanza seems this poem's antithesis
But it gives the whole idea proper synthesis
Combined we think differently, like varietal wines
Be on the same page, color outside the lines

Alone in the Dark

Ever feel like you're alone in the dark?
The silent screams from a restless mind
Thoughts and emotions painfully stark
Thinking there's no one else of your kind

The secret is learning that we're all like you
We all go through the same things that you do
Seem to go it alone, but we're all together
Feelings are shown, birds of a feather

The real test isn't jacked up situations
It's how you adequately respond
Foundations of human relations
The deep-down brotherly bond

Ever feel like you're alone in a crowd?
The panic seeping from every pore
Screaming inside, but never aloud
Terrified to your very core

The secret is learning there's many like you
Who get nervous and jittery outside of their crew
Anxiety is just a brain with a coup
Just keep doing you and we'll have a breakthrough

For every crowd, and each pitch-black night
There's a caring hug and a morning light
For all the solace and anxious tomorrows
Reach out to us to assuage your sorrows

People care more than you know
Most of us are just looking to grow
Hopefully with you in tow
Bound together, we all will glow

I Can Breathe

I can breathe because randomly genetically blessed
Damn sure I'll bleed to go to war for the rest
Don't care about your money or the way that you're dressed
Until something takes your breath, we're on the same quest

I'm lucky I can speak for those who lack voice
Damn sure I'll go to war for those who lack choice
Of gender, skin tone, creed, religion or region
We are human, we are legion

I don't have to agree with how you live your life
But I agree that you deserve to live with zero strife
So long as you don't hurt people and use your brain
I promise all my strain to ease your pain

I can also speak to the flaws in the system
There's the bad eggs, and we obviously missed 'em
Spent 5 days in a Velcro moo-moo
For breathing honest and telling my true-true

Obviously, I haven't yet passed
But I did go to shit police class
I can breathe because my color is white
I can't breathe because this keeps me up all night

I can breathe and I'll make some noise
For those relieved of their human poise
I will march and I will rant
For those lacking breath, and those who can't

I inhale deep to type and write
I hold it in long to fight the fright
I breathe a final sigh into the deep black night
Hoping to high hell that we can end this plight

True Terror

Do you want to know what, to the core, scares me?
Mirrors, empty bottles, my mother and doctors
Blank pages, unread books, lacking a reason to be
The future, the past and the under the bed monsters

Being awake, trying to sleep and the painful mental creep
Addictions, afflictions and the waters of the deep
Saying too much, not saying enough, lacking cahones to take the leap
Taking the leap and breaking my legs in a broken, hobbled heap

Phone calls and voicemails when I can't control the outcome
Emails and text messages that play my heart with patterned strum
Writing poems because it relieves me of the numb
Feeling like the only thing in life that matters is income

My eyelids, commercials and pretending I don't cry
Police officers, snakes and pretending I don't lie
Shower drains, I don't get it either and there's no reason why
The quiet times alone when I think it's ok just to die

Blinking cursors with no words to fill the void
Awkward situations I can't seem to avoid
The myriad of times I can't elucidate why I'm annoyed
Every single time I get caught slipping like Freud

I'm not proud of any of this nonsense
But owning up to my fear created this content
Dealing with it all seems a bit daunting
But I make it my goal to hit my fears with a haunting

Honest Thoughts

The worst lies are the ones we tell ourselves
Alone in the dark wishing something could help
All of the turmoil placed like trophies on shelves
Adrift with the tide like seaweed and kelp

All of the thoughts, processed or not
Create bars like a prison, inside you just rot
Lost sight of the things for which you have fought
Hamilton's laughing, you're wasting your shot

I write fire poems, it's sort of a gift
Trying to connect, but it's a cognitive sift
Through the bullshit; my brain feels hella swift
Like the keys on both sides, I'm trying to shift

My perspective and lifestyle to focus on growth
It's not easy or fun, but this is my oath
Love people and solitude, just can't do both
But I'll focus on others, that is my troth

Honest comes forefront, I'm kind of a mess
Oil me olive, I need the cold press
Tired joke about checkers and chess
These stanzas are the way I confess

Like a Catholic in a weird little box
Hail Mary, the grace is worse than detox
I really love our dumb little talks
Time for a dime in the slot, change the jukebox

This poem is better than you want to admit
Hits with my truth, I'm not scared of my shit
In the court of my life, no need to acquit
I give you the real, my honest transmit

Words hit the page that isn't a page
But I'm not acting, all the world's a stage
That's William for you, a beautiful sage
Shake that spear and human engage

I'll leave you with this, I love people the most
Like cinnamon rolls, bacon, eggs, side of toast
It gets a bit weird, but I've not seen riposte
I can't wait for my special Comedy Central roast

Honester Thoughts

How long did that take you?
Half the long hand rotation
The flow zone's what makes you
Write with no hesitation

It scares me to look back
Overthink becomes real
Backspaced Riddick's Pitch Black
The Chronicles, true to feel

As a human, I'm scared
But I put up a front
I'm impaired, not prepared
But I won't stop my hunt

For ideas and emotions
And people to love
Kayak the oceans
No god above

Deity resides in you and in me
The flaws that we have are what set us free
To give away crappy tacos, transcendent philosophy
That's nerd words for a decent human way to be

I get down, like deep, dark and angry
Stared death in the face, the scythe is what greets me
I'll tell you a secret, I don't know how to be
Add up the elements one plus one equals three

Switch it to Marvel, one bad snap, no cap
Only one who is worthy, Mjolnir's power to tap
Black Widow's one hand you don't want to snap
Wasps and Ants won't matter if Groot has his sap

Oh, DC is more of your flow?
That Batman Begins, he's super you know
Oh no, that's the one guy, Kent that is Clark
Not the Wonderful Woman who lassos her mark

Lord of the Rings, you're crushing on Strider
King of the Kings, the sexy horse rider
Rudy carries the Wood, He's not freeing Willy
Yeah, 90s reference, you're not being silly

Light a candle, three wicks, Bed, Bath and Beyond
299 is the death toll from the Wick that is John
You killed his dog. I'd murder you too
The living baba yaga is coming for you

Why do these thoughts exhibit more truth?
Because I want you to smile and go back to your youth
Beaten to death with things that don't matter
The chatter is there, but it's shit dipped in batter

Broken Brain

Not really a dumb kid
Not a smart one either
Test scores always hid
That I was always neither

I hate humanity, but love the human
Give all my effort but withhold my soul
Most days I feel in that world with Truman
People observing me in my little bowl

Cerebral lubrication
For calm mental station
Necessary for real relation
To perpetuate grey matter vibration

I'll fuck up your cortex
With all the words and all the dishes
I'll hit you with a vortex
Feeding over 5000 with far fewer fishes

That's a terrible bible joke
Don't care if you're Christian woke
Just don't be a jerk
If you say something snarky
Use the emoji smirk

I see 19 sides of every beef
Please don't imagine any grief
Have a drink and have a laugh
Brain broke af, 666x daily gaffes

They fed me drugs
They fed me therapy
When I just needed the right hugs
And enough time to find the real me

I'm broken as fuck
I see this planet as just a bit off
Wherewithal to know of my luck
Even if other people scoff

Now we write, and now we cook
Feed the minds, and feel the souls
Click on Amazon and buy my book
Then swing by for a couple spring rolls

The broken brains are best by far
But my perspective is skewed
In truth, broken brains are all we are
Without all of us, all of us are screwed

Escape Your Brain

Drugs, Religion, Sex and Crime
Individually, they make me rhyme
Collectively, they've cost me time
4 lines in, I'm in my prime

PTSD and BP 2
My brain probably needs a coup
Schizho, Psycho, Brain askew
Only matters if it's you

Drugs will put you in a place
Lyrics missing, drop the bass
Hope to hell there is no lace
Dragon is what you chase

Maybe god will save you
Can you spell allahu?
If you're Hindu, don't kill cow, moo
Christian single? Sorry, you can't screw

Think is that which I do most
Hope it turns me to a ghost
I wait for one useful riposte
Pushing slow the lethal dose

A-A rhyming makes me tired
Loss of brain is what's required
Hired, fired, just to be desired
Tough words are always admired

Stepping out is painful, much
If you're G-Eazy, chop a Dutch
Blame no one, there is no crutch
You are you, just act as such

Drugs, Religion, Sex and Crime
Most are better in your prime
Poem coming to a climb
Peace of mind is the sublime

Problem is we can't have just one
If we could, we'd all be done
As is this verse, this shit is spun
All shots fired, yet no handgun

100 Proof

Strong liquor makes it quicker
Here's the stickler and the kicker
Makes the ticker flit and flicker
Blood trickles a little slicker

Pour that Maker's Mark
Crack a triple IPA
Let it give your brain a spark
And swallow your life away

Care about a Malbec
Or Tempranillo of the day
Give that silly brain a wreck
All you want is just a way

To think a little less
And do a little more
Alleviate some stress
Grab a couple snores

You worry about truth
People worry about you
Doesn't take a sleuth
To pick up on the clue

I'm Jack from the Shining
Stephen King is pining
Nicholson is whining
Liquor levels declining

100 is the test score
That gets you to the liquor store
Where gain becomes pain
21 of age playing with pure grain

I will wink, and I'll nod
I'll smile quite odd
We all meet our ends
Have 100 proof friends

I love everyone, I hope you do too
Proof, percentage, mixed or not
Have some fun, and be true
Be safe, find a ride, and do only you

The Prelude

The last sip hits, and you already know the future
Dry heaves that rip far too deep to suture
Fearing bites of food, feigning smiles to hide your mood
Wanting to dismiss yourself from life, but you don't want to be rude

Self-inflicted harm works a charm
Until it begins to sound alarm
But at that point, there's no reverse
You've doomed yourself to Montezuma's curse

It gets hard to breathe just as you want to sleep
But now you're in deep and can't count enough sheep
Then the reflux starts, burning all your heart
The chronic cough tastes of blood, the very worst part

Lie to yourself, say it's your last detox
But therein lies the problem of Pandora's box
This process is your religion now
And younger you just doesn't get how

It got to this level and the total cost
Licenses, savings, relationships lost
And you'd do it again, the entire affliction
Because that's the real issue, your addiction to addiction

True Addiction

I fill a glass because of habit
Some chase dragons, mine's a rabbit
Wake up messed up. "Tomorrow's gonna suck"
The hole we run down, is where we get stuck

It's a string, means it resonates
Ride the wave 'til it detonates
We act like animals, full on primates
But fate waits at pearly gates

That's the crash, full backlash
The ones you love, left with your trash
All your people writhe and thrash
It's your wreck, your balderdash

That means we choose it; we do at first
Then it's ritual; and then you're cursed
Tragedy must quench your thirst
For one hot moment, then verse reversed

Solace in things that comfort brings
Unaware of the chorus that ballad sings
Mom picks up the phone that rings
Coroner tones of angel's wings

Addiction is a flashlight
Into personal insight
Your fears at night
Now broad daylight

When it becomes true
Neutralizes you
Baptizes you
Capsizes you

Requiem in Rhyme

Equilibrium point, morning joint
Internal counterpoint to disappoint
The oil anoint of the odd disjoint
Background issue without pinpoint

True addiction is addiction to addiction
The love of things that derive affliction
Voracity without eviction
Losing corporeal jurisdiction

When odd becomes normal, open a case
When the rabbit you're chasing's winning the race
When the vocals fade out and dude drops the bass
When your main point of thought is going to space

I can write this because this dude is me
When this dude is awake, he just wants to be free
Of his brain and emotion, turmoil and guilt
But all of this mess warms like a quilt

Waking Up

I hate the way I woke up today
Sleep'll be 56 hours away
Everything I do pushes other astray
Dumb words with hope to make it okay

I live in a place I love but doesn't feel home
I do all these things I love but I feel like I roam
I try to fix the things in encoded genome
But damn if I don't feel I'm my own catacomb

They want metaphors because a poem, it makes
Quatrains the gas and just miss the brakes
Perspective's a bitch and hot sand it breaks
Metaphor the collision, petit four is your cake

I've never done a thing well in my life
Outside of cause great people strife
Better words written from a chimp with a knife
I should probably join Thoreau out in wildlife

Everything I have not to run
Everything I have not to quit
I just want to be done
I hate that all that I am isn't it

Positivity is my goal
But sometimes reality wins
I want to hit you with my soul
Because I was trained to think in sins

Depression

This one hits home
With more than a few
You don't hit depression
Depression hits you

Awake all night
Lay in bed all day
Nothing feels right
Make it go away

Drink too much
Swallow narcotics
It's all a crutch
That makes us robotic

Tunnels all end
You don't have to
Injuries mend
Let's talk it through

Platitudes aside
It feels all too much
You've cried, died yet tried
To come through in the clutch

You're not alone
And nothing can stop you
Apply skills you can hone
You'll find what you knew

Everything ends
Depression can today
Friends pay dividends
Make today your life day

I Love You ⎯⎯⎯⎯⎯⎯⎯⎯⎯⎯⎯⎯

I love you for the smiles you bring
I love you for the songs that you sing
I love you for the thoughts that you ping
I love you for every god damn thing
I love you for the comments that sting
I love you for a fling that turned to a ring

I love you through tears
I love you through fears
I love you through my ears
I love you through wine and beers
I love you through dinner cheers
I love you through all the years

I love you for your terrible dance
I love you for making me advance
I love you with green eggs in France
I loved you with a single glance
I loved you on random ass chance
I love you with a future advance

I love it when you beat me at games
I love it when we put photos in frames
I love it when we talk about our aims
I love it that we're each other's claims
I love it when we chill by the flames
I love when rhymes run out, Lebron James

I love you for merging lives
I love you for bad joke high fives
I love you for respecting my knives
I love that this poem is in the archives
I love that you always pick up some chives
I love that you'll be the very best of wives

REQUIEM IN RHYME

I love that you call me on my shit
I love that you call me just to spit
I love that you have zero quit
I love that you make me commit
I love that you make me admit
That sometimes I'm a wreck just a bit

I love that you allow me to fail
I love that I'll see you in a veil
I love when your face makes mine go pale
I love sending poems to your secret email
I love that you read me blind, like braille
I love that together, we make quite the tale

I love that tomorrow will be better than today
I love that we're good in this, come what may
I love that if demons spawn, we'll slay
I love knowing, when tired, where to lay
I love it when we work hard, and def when we play
I love that you're my everyday

Bottle Metaphor

Pop the top, apprehensive
Take a whiff, feeling pensive
Pour a bit into the glass
Mix it well, sip with class

Unpleasant at first
But it grows on you
Quenching your thirst
You're happy. It's true.

A full drink in, feeling fine
No way have you crossed the line
Dance and sing; laugh and smile
You won't realize it for a while

Has it been 2 hours, or maybe 5 years?
A quarter bottle in, but still having fun
You're under its powers, nights end in tears
Going full throttle, thinking you've won

Woah, you're halfway there
Woah-oh mom's saying a prayer
Meanwhile, your pockets are bare
Fill that glass and wake up somewhere

Tell yourself you're living the life
Tell yourself you've got no more strife
Tell yourself that it's just a phase
Tell yourself you're not lost in a haze

You tip past half and the weight starts to change
Your memory gets fuzzy and your actions are strange
The prioritized thoughts in your head rearrange
You begin to question if you might be deranged

REQUIEM IN RHYME

You've reached three fourths, drinking liquor, cheap
One fourth of the person you wanted to keep
Feels like more than a decade you've been asleep
Not even drunken nights, just mental upkeep

You think about more and forget about most
Ingest a swig to become a broken ghost
An empty shell with nothing to give
A piece of shit with no right to live

Woah, you're almost there
Woah-oh you're saying a prayer
Meanwhile, your pantry is bare
Hide that glass and fake it everywhere

Now you're drinking alone
Swilling it straight
On your own on the throne
Empty bottle magnate

Raise a handle to the sky
See right through to the moon
Realize, if you don't try
You'll be eclipsed quite soon

The grip of addiction now physical
Forgot how you got here, it's quizzical
The cramps and the sweats til you shake
The dry heaves and no sleeps til you break

Woah, you made it there
Woah-oh you didn't need a prayer
Now your pockets and pantry are bare
Dump that glass, help is out there

See, the bottom of the bottle isn't the end
You must empty it, to fill it again
Know it won't be easy to transcend
But there's no better time to begin

The bottle metaphor is finally tapped
Wait that's a keg, mind finally snapped
You just need to find a new way to be
Because the You in this poem is Me

What's Wrong

'What's wrong?' Is what they always ask
No one's ever been keen to the task
Of pass rushing my broken brain
Or intercepting my mental pain

'What's wrong?' would take a couple years
A couple pills and a couple tears
A couple moments to explain my fears
A couple bottles and a couple beers

'You're, intelligent, handsome with so much to give'
Yet I sit alone in the dark not wanting to live
'You crack jokes, and laugh; always have a good time'
Then people go home so I sit here and rhyme

'What's wrong?' Know this is true
I'd fix that shit, if I only just knew
It's not like a revelation out of the blue
Hard to fathom if the person ain't you

'What's wrong?' Mental, physical, emotional pain
My feeling of human beginning to drain
Please, someone disconnect my brain
I honestly believe I'm going insane

What's wrong is being told it's not normal
Your feelings and notions a bit out of line
Being dismissed, nonchalant and informal
Because your mind and theirs aren't aligned

What's wrong is being forced to conform
By people who could never brainstorm
Adequate ways to help you transform
If you don't fit the mold, you have to reform

What's wrong is all of life's bullshit excuses
For dismissing people who don't fill your uses
Differences are what bring us together
Counterintuitive intelligence, forever

What's wrong is most words, written or spoken
Fall on deaf ears with cognition broken
It's harder to think than it is to just live
Like it's easier to take than be open and give

What's wrong is usually nothing at all
Most of us just lost in the crawl
Beating our heads against the wall
Waiting for the inevitable downfall

I Need Help

I need help for stress and anxiety
I need help for the demons inside of me
I need help for elevated BAC
I need help to sleep for hours more than 3

I need help for the kids that don't have lunches
I need help for the poor that die in bunches
On floor mattresses with no box springs
Pulling deeply at my heart strings

I need help for the beautiful-souled queer
I need help for people cutting due to fear
Of walking out the door just to hear the jeers
To walk right back inside just to hide the tears

I need help to stop having perspective
I need help finding the objective
Of silly words on broken lines
When all that matters is broken minds

I need help for the firefighting crew
I need help for me, and I need help for you
To be the best we can for all those who cannot
Even if in the end, forgot and for naught

I need help for the jobless single mom
I need help for the teen with backpack bomb
Dogmatized and weaponized for other's wealth
Not realizing all they've done is jeopardize their health

I need help for all the strung out, struggling addicts
I need help for those who sleep on benches or bricks
Hoping that next scratch off may get them an apartment
When odds are better it's a police department

I need help for all the things left unsaid
I need help for those stuck inside their head
With broken thoughts and wasted youth
Searching for some impossible truth

I need help to not fake smile
I need help to stay a while
For all the folks who've seen me through
And all the faces I'll meet brand new

I need help for the homeless vet
I need help for the family pet
Both have matter, both have meaning
All they need is intervening

I need help for silent fears
I need help for fallen tears
Down faces of people just like me
That just haven't found the way to be

We all need help every now and then
So just reach out and be a friend
To all those jerks you meet and greet
You'll never know when you'll be on the street

Satisfaction of Delusion

Mirror, truth, illuminates but one
Shining light, internal thought yet spun
Reflects bright, yet hopeful true
One idyllic, perfect you

The truth we tell is oft our own
Actual fact, never known
Smiles deep down to the core
Lies internal, more and more

Happy seems the bright facade
Masses laugh, awed, we're fraud
Carry on the odd charade
Happy, but integrally flawed

Sleeping well more times than naught
Such nice winks are often bought
With notions faulty to the plot
Matters not, attention caught

One day we'll wake up to the truth
Wish we did more with our youth
In our last and dying days
See the folly of our ways

Wake up dead
Find out fast
Silly heads
Never last

Ignorance, please find quite bliss
Now tonight, give loving kiss
To what you think your happy life
Tomorrow owned by one sharp knife

Final Moment

Hello creature, why are you here?
This is heaven, right? I've had a bible for years.
You think omnipotence has these gates 'cause of fear?
Don't think that at all, it's the land of no tears.

If I open gates pearly, what merits your streets of gold?
I rose early for church, sang hymns and read the stories of old.
Says here you tipped three percent, and stiffed the valet
And a homeless man ignored to smell a bridesmaid's bouquet?

Omniscience says you masturbated 4 score and then we invented commas.
But then I went on a mission trip and sowed seed to half the Bahamas.
You raped 19 kids, and dolled up for interviews on Sundays.
But I asked for forgiveness. Repentance perpetual Mondays.

Satan led the angels; you think you get in on some word play?
Believe in your heart; isn't that what the words say?
They also talk about slavery, shellfish and horse jizz
21st century taxation, lobster and cheese whiz

Shut the fuck up, you're not getting into heaven
Ok, yeah it sucks, but salvation isn't bread that's unleavened
Absolution comes from getting everything right here
Except you never will, and the globe's not a right sphere

Look, this poem doesn't make me happy
And I hope to high hell it makes you mad
These topics make me scrappy
But I don't really feel bad

When I piss off pious people
Who claim to speak from highest mountains
We don't need your steeple
We need to quench thirst from our own fountains

REQUIEM IN RHYME

So yeah, I'm an asshole, not worthy of heaven
But I'll drain my wallet at 7-11
Before anyone in my sphere feels like a peasant
I commit to this life and to be fucking present

So judge me according to the book of your choosing
My flesh can take bruising, but I'm the one using
The tools at my disposal to dispelll all the nonsense
But if it makes you feel better, put your shit in the comments

Angel and Demon

A's in the class
Liquor in the glass
Laughter in the dead of night
Success that comes from penning right

Seeking help for broken brain
Feeling untold amounts of pain
You don't need a lobotomy
Just need to lose dichotomy

All things have potential
Perspective is essential
To weigh the good and bad
The happy and the sad

Angel in the morning
Demon round 'bout 10
You never get the warning
On when it's hell or when it's Zen

Monday a saint
Wednesday a monster
Friday, no complaints
Sunday, an imposter

Here's the thing that's not often said
Most binary rules have been placed in your head
Only you have the power to think for yourself
Some of the nonsense belongs on the shelf

Things will look luscious
But they also may crush us
Things will look average
When they may make us savage

Satan himself started out at the top
Just waiting on the DJ to make the beat drop
So all of the angels could fly on a wing
And all the new demons could torment something

Don't measure life on 0s and 1s
Our existence isn't binary
Angel or demon, know I love you tons
And we all need a bit of refinery

What fills your wallet
Isn't in your heart
I don't care how you call it
Angel or demon, you're a damn work of art

Fear

Afraid to tell the truth
Afraid to tell a lie
Afraid to lose our youth
Afraid to not know why

Afraid of the known, yet also unknown
Afraid of being known yet also not 'known'
Afraid of precious seconds ticking by
Afraid of thinking of all the ways to die

Afraid of corrupt government
Afraid of wasted money spent
Afraid of any texts left unread
Afraid of all the things left unsaid

Afraid of emails and phone calls missed
Afraid your ideas might be dismissed
Afraid to slit your wrist
Afraid to cease to exist

Afraid for people suffering hunger
Afraid none of us are getting younger
Afraid for people who suffer with addiction
Afraid for people who read shitty fiction

5 stanzas of fear, that's quite enough
As of late, we've had enough of that stuff
Sometimes life gets a little tough
But let's rebuff with a chuff and call life's bluff

Time to flip the script a little bit
Roll fear up and take a hit
All to fear is fear itself
Nailed it my dude, Roosevelt

REQUIEM IN RHYME

Not afraid to speak my mind
Not afraid of being kind
Not afraid of being weird
Not afraid of greying, sexy beard

Not afraid of what you think
Not afraid to make you think
Not afraid to pour us drinks
Not afraid to see a shrink

Not afraid of good police
Not afraid of a riot release
Not afraid to be a voice
Not afraid to give you choice

Not afraid to write my words
Not afraid to go unheard
Not afraid of feedback, hard swallowing
Not afraid to build a small following

Not afraid to be your friend
Not afraid to slightly offend
Not afraid to give fear a breather
Not afraid to love you either

That's five stanzas of fear rebuttal
Fear loses this scuttle and it's not very subtle
Fear is what you let it be
So don't let it breathe

We're all in this mess together
We're all in this mess forever
Hell, highwater, whatever weather
With our heads right, fear affects us never

Deeply Flawed

First iterations, often horribly wrong
Initial lyrics, not a perfect song
Flaws are what make art, art
The slight mistakes do their part

To make the overall creation
A thing to appreciate
From those of human relation
Who produce and carry their weight

The greatest of minds
Have broken synapses, too
But it often reminds
They're also in you

Cracks may point out spots that are weak
But also, opportunities to become strong
Through hard work, repair, or perspective tweak
We patch up our walls with changes, lifelong

You may suffer from issues outside your control
Those defects make you a beautiful soul
Perfection isn't what makes you whole
I'll extol how imperfections play the role

In making you the powerful person you are
Without mine, you don't get these bars
Made of remnants from ancient, flawed stars
We're all evidence of cosmic scars

Without those flaws, we wouldn't be graced
With the ones you possess or your beautiful face
So display 'em on a shelf, make it a showcase
And your fear of them will start to erase

REQUIEM IN RHYME

We'll look at your bookcase and quickly applaud
For the person that hides them is truly a fraud
Don't be the one who disappears behind a facade
At the end of the day please be Deeply Flawed

Living on the Inside

The click of the keys becomes part of me
Push on the springs and they rebound and sing
Echo mental reverb in a melancholy key
Riding the wave, crests before every downswing

Trapped in a prison, meat sack of cells in a cell
Inside lies hell, outside doing well
An inner need to thrash and rebel
To be the golden yolk that breaks its own shell

Religion is the thing that taught me to lie
It beats you to death with shame
Omit the truth, to elders satisfy
Notch a win in eternal blame game

Mysterious answers to questions unasked
Causing even the supple to calcify
Don't pose real queries, they can't be unmasked
Because they know their rebuttals will petrify

'We don't know' is what they should say
Instead, we're hit with conjecture
Parables and anecdotes day after day
Lecture cripples brain architecture

Breaking the law made me a criminal
Judication tripled the threat
In the moment existence was pivotal
Left alone while they hedged on their bet

Now I'm left to cover the debt
Of my actions, while taking on others'
I say what I think, that makes me a threat
All for my brothers, my druthers

REQUIEM IN RHYME

Mothers with prudence, I caution you this
Raise them up in the way they should go
With cognitive prison, you're remiss
Don't shackle minds that could glow

To those of you out there who feel quite like me
Convinced you've committed unforgiveable sin
You don't need a lawyer, lockpick or key
All mental doors are locked from within

Sunset Fades

I like to watch the sunset
Because my home is in the dark
When the sky fades from rage to dark brunette
It speaks directly to my heart

Not evil or nefarious, just enjoy the solemn silence
It's the tidal wave that grants a symbolistic island
When shores box you in, waves remain the only violence
It strips you of your license, you remain the only tyrant

I like the idea of moving east
Wheels fight the time the least
Sky shades invoke your own
Polarized but in the zone

Rose tinted glasses turn a bit more jade
When the music starts to fade
And the ball of fusion drifts out of sight
Comfort comes with every night

In truth, I prefer to wander west
My destiny is manifest
Which feels empty for today
All these words, with nothing real to say

Thinking Without Thinking

Thinking without thinking started this thing
Doing the same, I thought it a fling
Thinking without thinking brought a smile to your face
And in doing so, it made my heart race

Now I think without thinking of all that we are
Happy hour at the bar, bad karaoke in the car
I think without thinking of what the future holds
Absolutely enthralled for all that unfolds

I think without thinking about your scent in the air
Also making your coffee and your hair everywhere
I think without thinking about your goofy fake laugh
On your internal calls when you gab with your staff

I think without thinking about how you've helped me to grow
As a person who just lives to be your hero
I think without thinking how I fall short for you
Know I take it all personal, too

Thinking without thinking as you snore in the dark
Is one of the best things that ever touched my heart
As I think without thinking, your existence causes a spark
Illuminating for me that we never can part

Thinking without thinking of what's next for dinner
Knowing it won't matter, with you I'm a winner
Thinking without thinking of the kitty and pup
They're in it with us and we're not giving up

Thinking without thinking can be a strange notion
I need it for tranquility in my crazy brain ocean
Thinking without thinking is the stuff that comes natural
This rhyme isn't perfect, but you are, it's factual

Thinking without thinking about travels abroad
And all the times I let you rant and just nod
Thinking without thinking helps me know it's all true
And very most of all that I'm in love with you

www.ingramcontent.com/pod-product-compliance
Lightning Source LLC
LaVergne TN
LVHW011858060526
838200LV00054B/4405